piano • vocal • guitar

T0087817

rob thomas

...something to be

ISBN 1-4234-0094-1

HAL•LEONARD®
CORPORATION
7777 W. BLUEMOUND RD. P.O. BOX 13819 MILWAUKEE, WI 53213

In Australia Contact:
Hal Leonard Australia Pty. Ltd.
4 Lentara Court
Cheltenham, Victoria, 3192 Australia
Email: ausadmin@halleonard.com

Visit Hal Leonard Online at
www.halleonard.com

THIS IS HOW A HEART BREAKS

Words and Music by ROB THOMAS,
CHRISTIAN KARLSSON, PONTUS WINNBERG
and HENRIK JONBACK

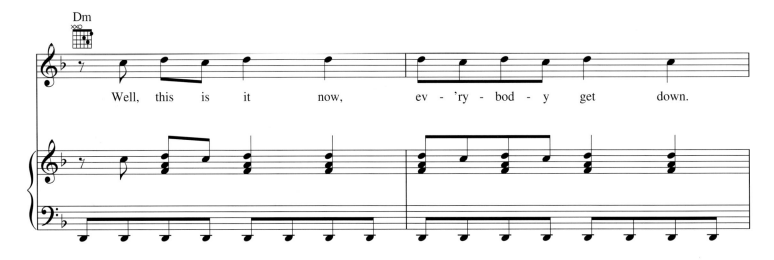

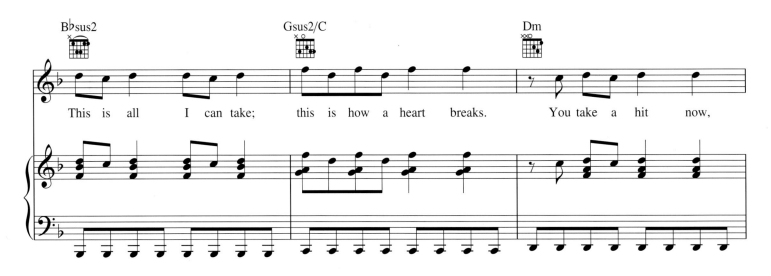

you feel it break down, make you stay wide a-wake. This is how a heart breaks.

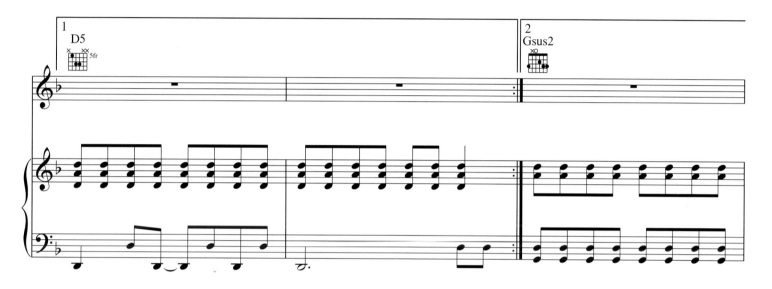

Well, this is how a heart breaks.

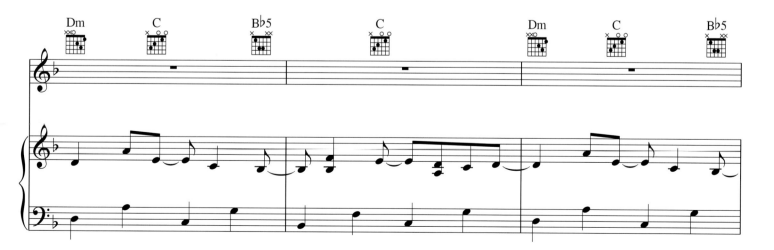

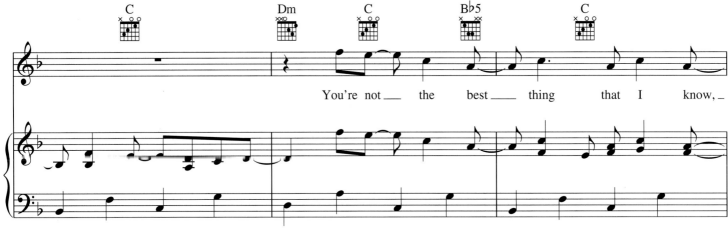

You're not ___ the best ___ thing that I know, ___

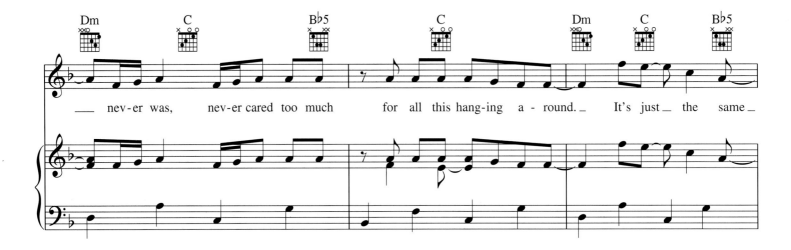

___ nev-er was, nev-er cared too much for all this hang-ing a - round. ___ It's just ___ the same ___

___ thing all the time: ___ nev-er get what I want, nev-er get too close to the end of the line. ___

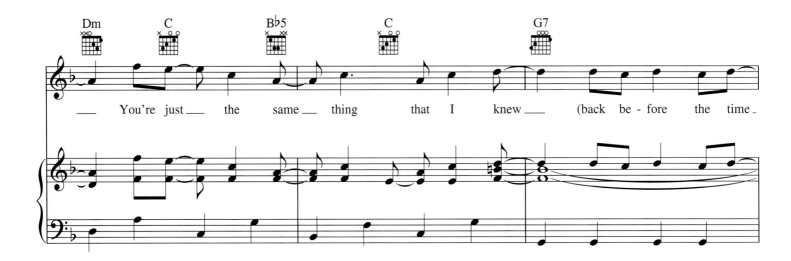

___ You're just ___ the same ___ thing that I knew ___ (back be - fore the time ___

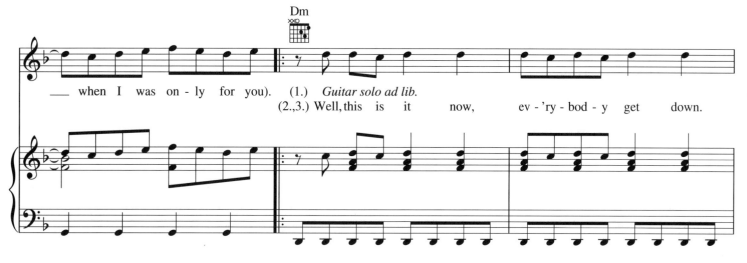

when I was on - ly for you). (1.) *Guitar solo ad lib.*
(2.,3.) Well, this is it now, ev - 'ry - bod - y get down.

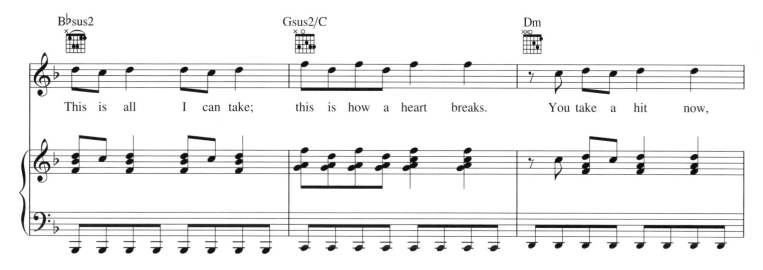

This is all I can take; this is how a heart breaks. You take a hit now,

Play 3 times

you feel it break down, make you stay wide a - wake. This is how a heart breaks.

LONELY NO MORE

Words and Music by
ROB THOMAS

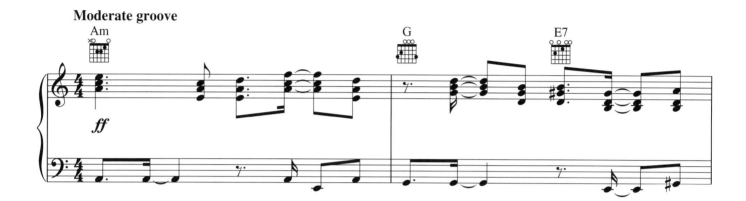

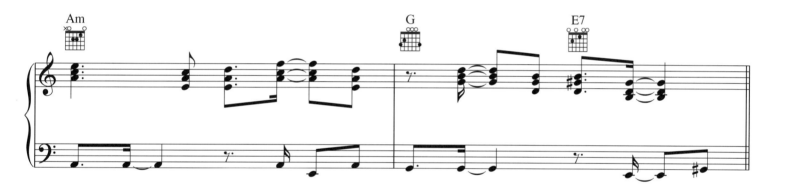

Now it seems __ to me __ that you know __ just what to say. __

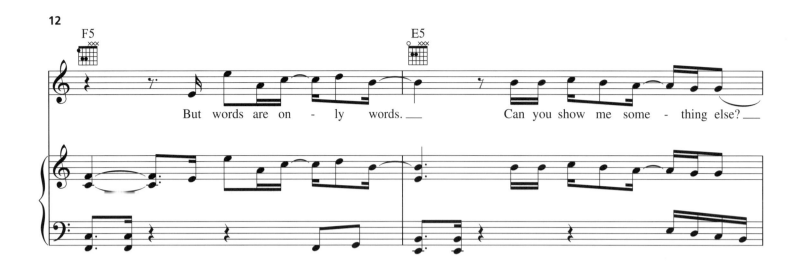

But words are on - ly words. ___ Can you show me some - thing else? ___

___ Can you swear ___ to me ___ that you'll al - ways be ___ this way?

Show me how ___ you ___ feel ___ more than ev - er, ba - by, ba - by, ba - by, ba - by.

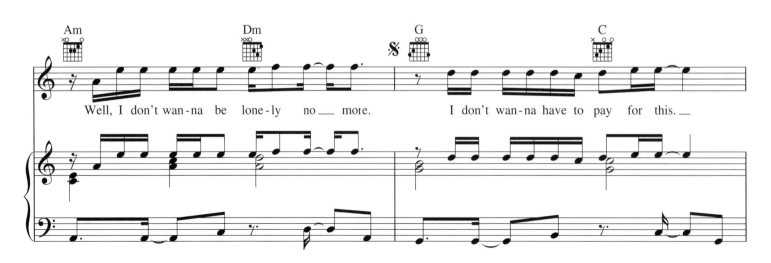

Well, I don't wan-na be lone-ly no ___ more. I don't wan-na have to pay for this. ___

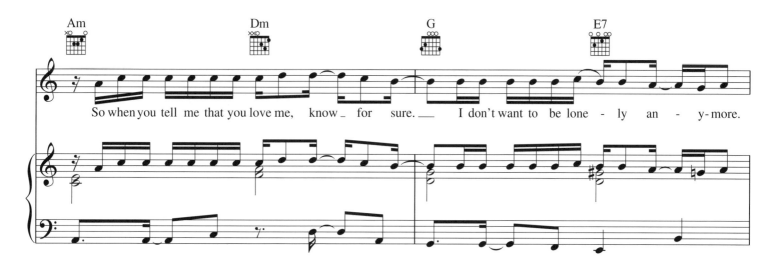

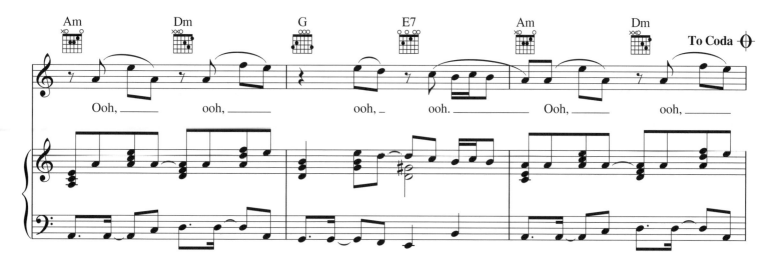

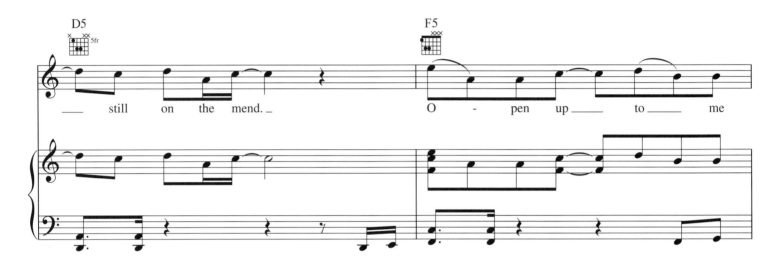

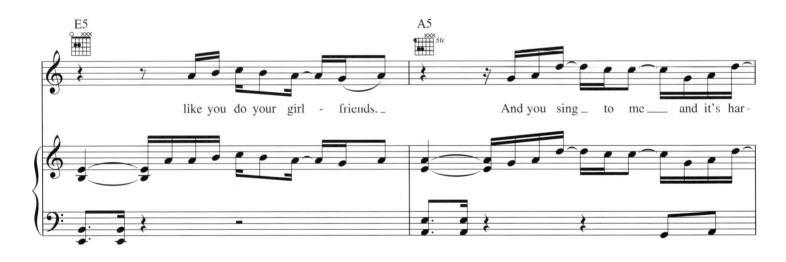

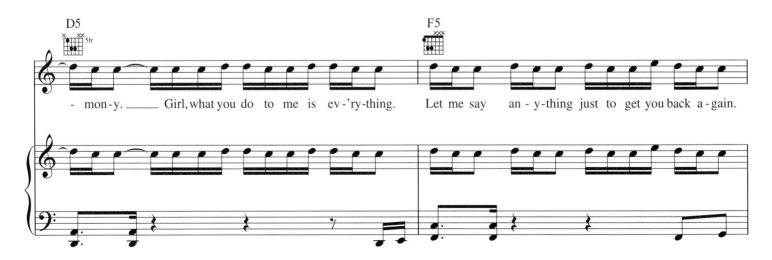

D.S. al Coda

Why can't we just try. I don't wan-na be lone-ly no ___ more.

ooh. ___ What if I was good to you? ___ What if you were

good to me? What if I could hold you 'til I feel ___ you move ___ in - side ___

___ of me? ___ And what if it was par - a - dise? ___ And what if we ___

_____ were sym-pho-nies? _____ What if I _____ gave all _____ my life _____ to

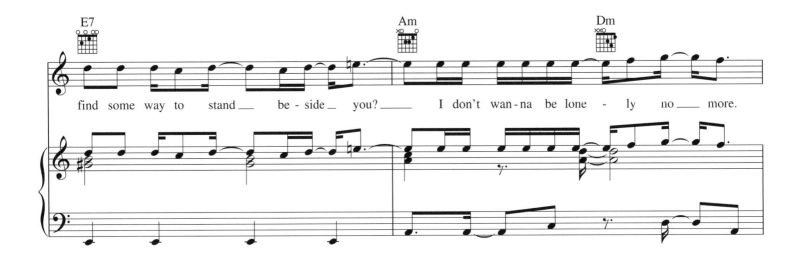

find some way to stand _____ be-side _____ you? _____ I don't wan-na be lone - ly no _____ more.

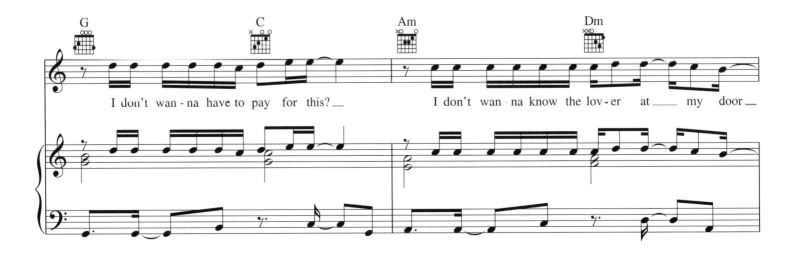

I don't wan-na have to pay for this? _____ I don't wan-na know the lov-er at _____ my door _____

_____ is just an-oth-er heart-ache on _____ my list. _____ I don't wan-na be an - gry no _____ more.

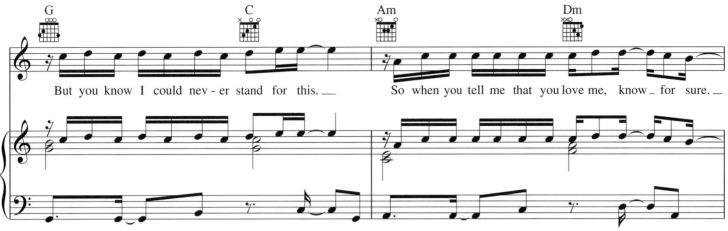

But you know I could nev-er stand for this. ___ So when you tell me that you love me, know ___ for sure. __

___ I don't wan-na be lone - ly an - y-more. Ooh, _____ ooh, _____ ooh, _ ooh. _____

(Lead vocal ad lib. on repeat)

___ ooh, _____ ___ ooh, _____ I don't wan-na be lone - ly an - y-more.

Repeat and Fade

Optional Ending

EVER THE SAME

Words and Music by
ROB THOMAS

*Recorded a half step lower.

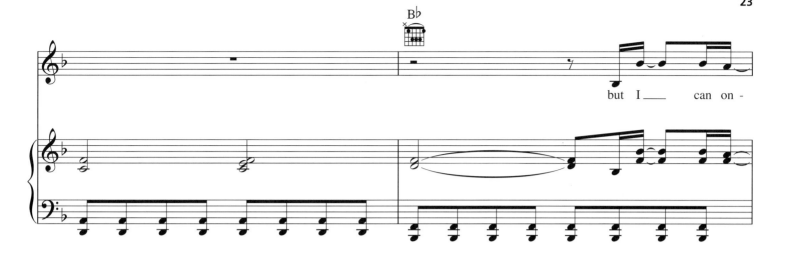

but I ___ can on -

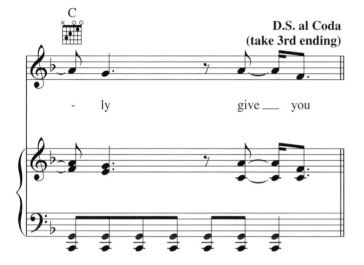

D.S. al Coda
(take 3rd ending)

CODA

- ly give ___ you

For - ev - er ___ with you, ___

___ for - ev - er ___ in me, ev - er ___

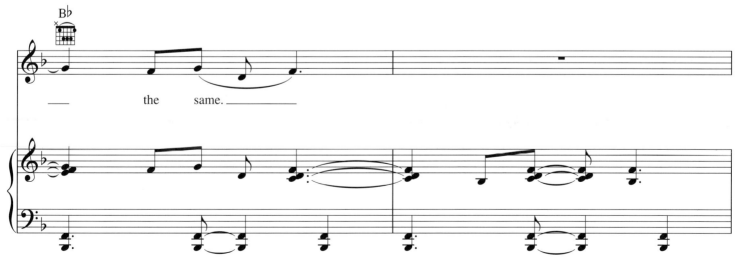

___ the same. _____

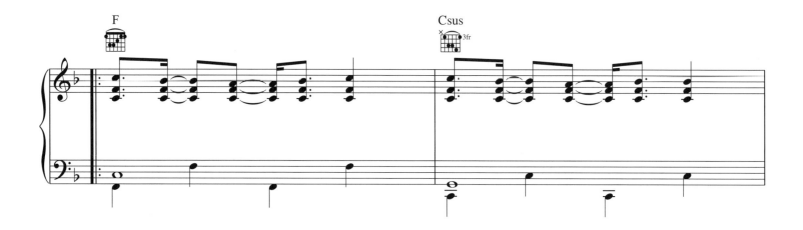

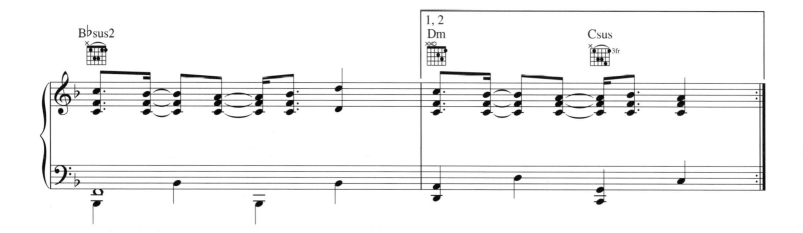

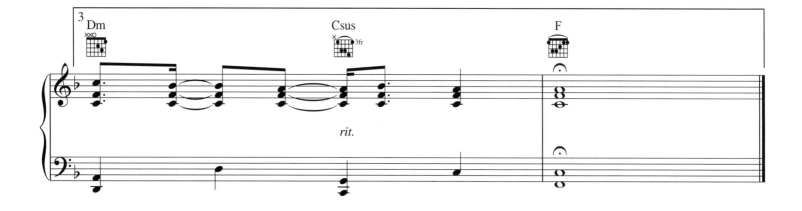

I AM AN ILLUSION

Words and Music by
ROB THOMAS

Moderately fast

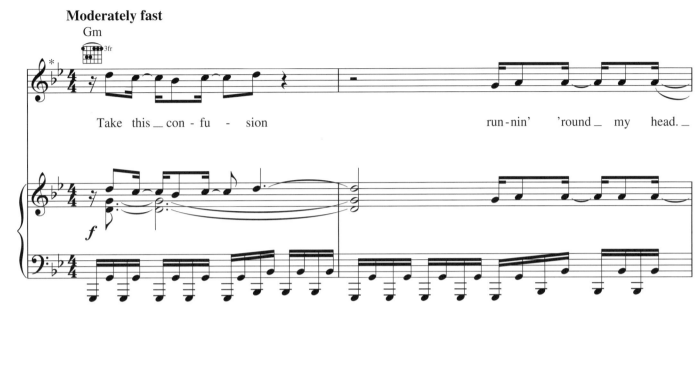

Take this __ con - fu - sion   run-nin' 'round __ my head. __

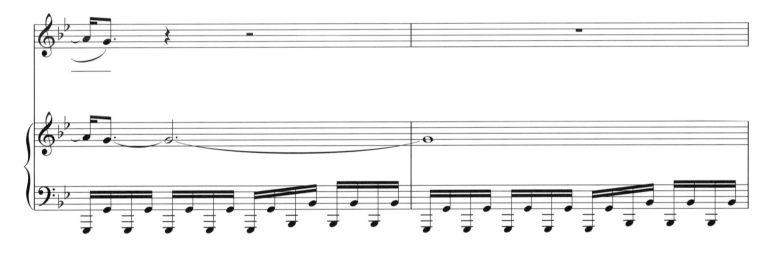

Take back __ my un - kind words;   lay that weight __ on me __

* *Recorded a half step higher.*

in - stead.

I'm the place where ev - 'ry - thing___ turns___

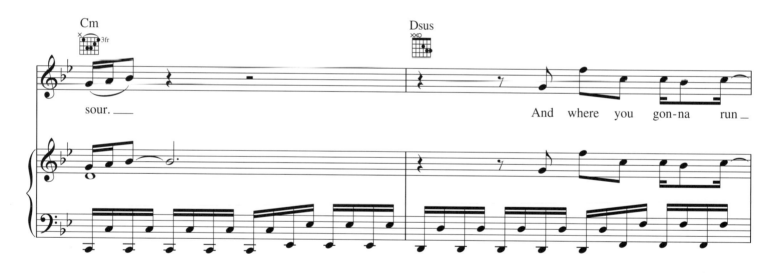

sour. ___ And where you gon-na run _

___ to now? _

real __ an-y-more: __ I am an il-lu-

-sion. Well, I'm not

real ___ an-y-more: ___ I am an il-lu-

-sion.

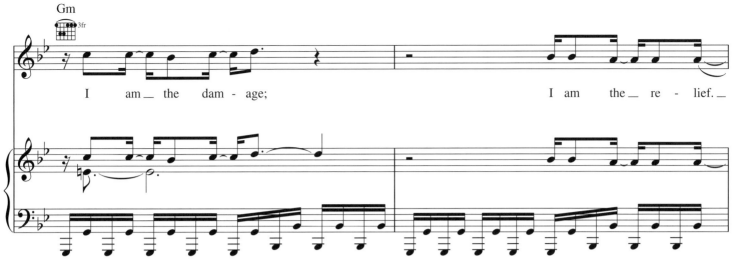

I am __ the dam - age; I am the __ re - lief. __

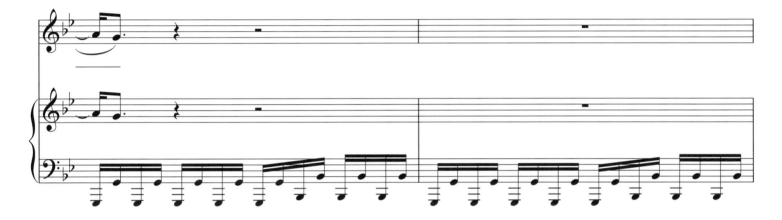

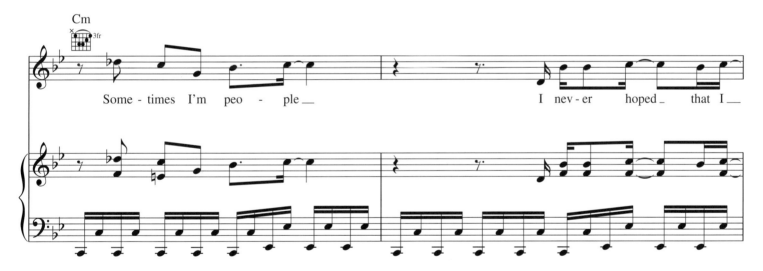

Some - times I'm peo - ple __ I nev - er hoped __ that I __

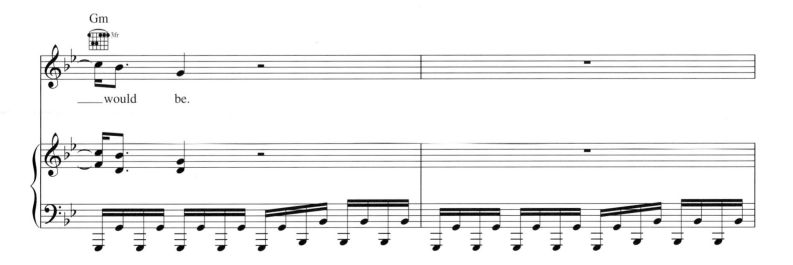

__ would be.

If I take in what-ev - er they ___ turn ___ out,

then what's that gon-na make ___

___ me now? ___ Don't you un - der - stand, ___ hell, I'm ___ not

real ___ an - y - more: ___ I am an il - lu -

- sion. Hell, I'm not

Cm11

real ___ an - y - more. ___ I am an il - lu-

Gm6

- sion.

Dm   Cm

D.S. al Coda

CODA

Hell, I'm ___ not real ___ an - y - more. _____

I am an il - lu - sion.

Got-ta help ___ me; I'm ___ not real ___ an - y - more. _____

I am an il - lu - sion.

One (one), two (two), three (three), four (four)!

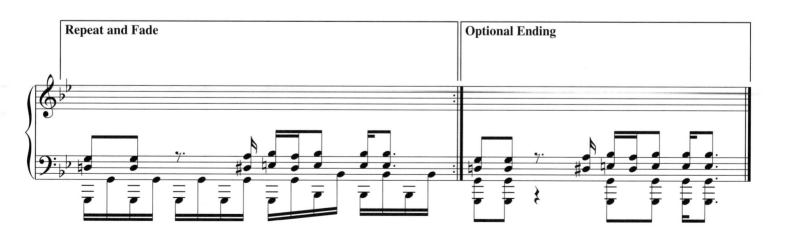

Repeat and Fade

Optional Ending

WHEN THE HEARTACHE ENDS

Words and Music by
ROB THOMAS

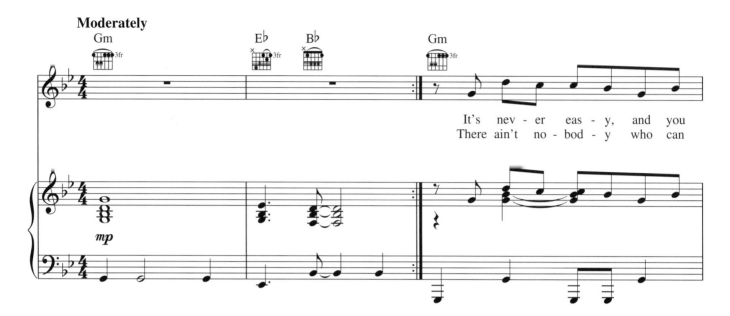

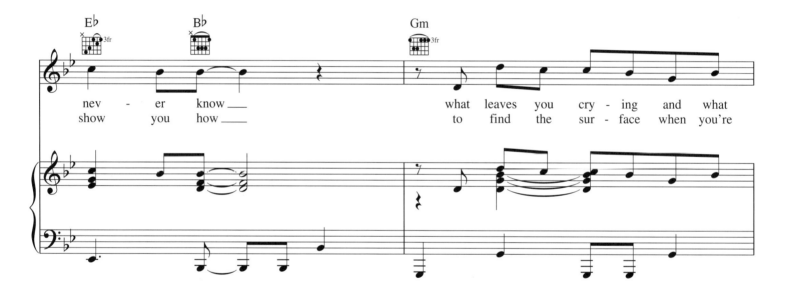

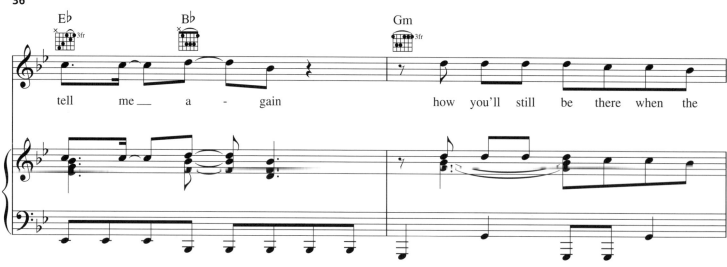

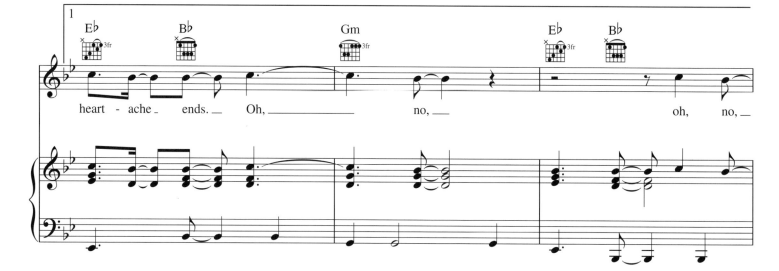

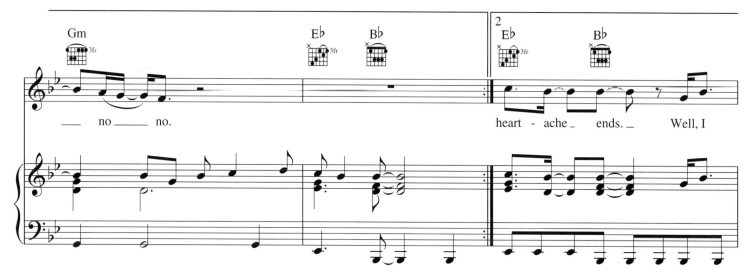

Eb

-ers and the lone - ly start to whis - per all a-bout__ me, and if I

Bbsus   Bb   Bbsus   Bb

stand here __ si - lent I al - most start to feel __ you fad - ing

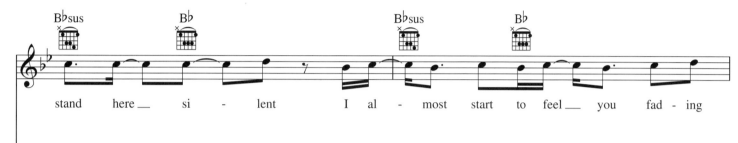

F

in,   tell - ing me, __ "Hold on," __ 'cause it's gon-na be

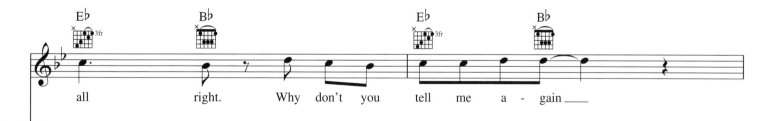

Eb   Bb   Eb   Bb

all   right.   Why don't you tell me a - gain __

SOMETHING TO BE

Words and Music by
ROB THOMAS

Hey man, I don't wan-na hear a-bout love no more. I don't wan-na talk a-bout

how I feel. I don't real-ly wan-na be ___ me, no, ___ no ___ more. ___

Lyrics:

I can't stand what I'm start-ing to be, no, I can't stand the peo-ple that I'm start-ing to meet. There's so ___ much now ___ that can go wrong, ___ and I don't ___ need no-bod-y try'in' to help it a-long. It's the same ___ old ___ song: ___ ev-'ry-bod-y says you've been a-

way too long;   ev-'ry-bod-y wan-na tell you   what   went wrong, wan-na make you like an   i - con

'til   you   be - lieve   that they're right.   I've   been   look - ing   for   some -

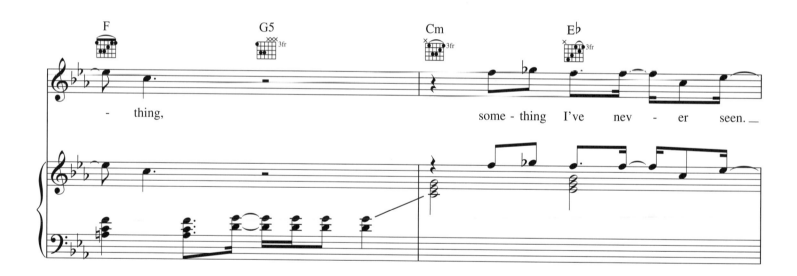

- thing,   some - thing I've nev - er seen. __

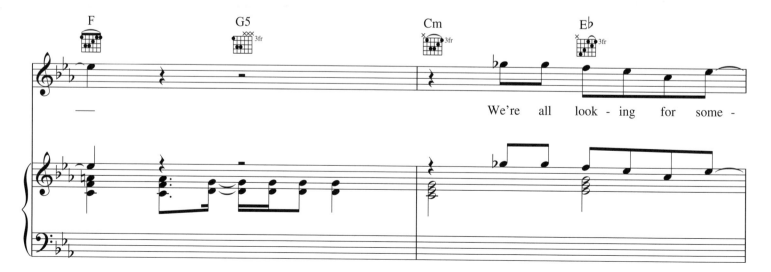

__   We're all look - ing for some -

Yeah,   yeah,   yeah. ___

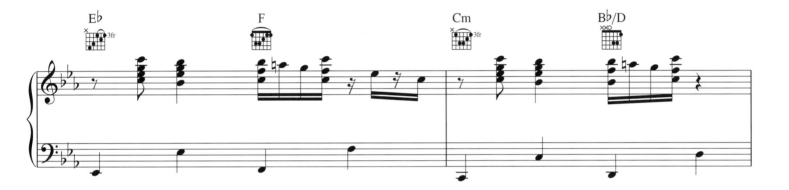

Yeah,   yeah,   yeah. ___ *(Vocal 1st time only)*

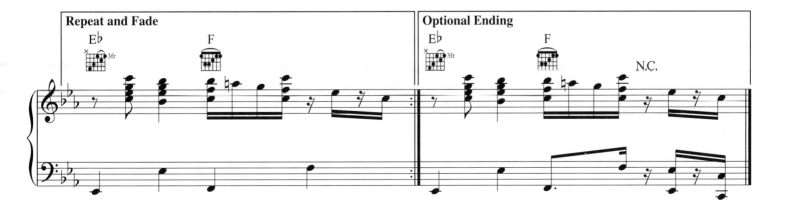

Repeat and Fade

Optional Ending

N.C.

ALL THAT I AM

Words and Music by
ROB THOMAS

Yeah, yeah, yeah. ____

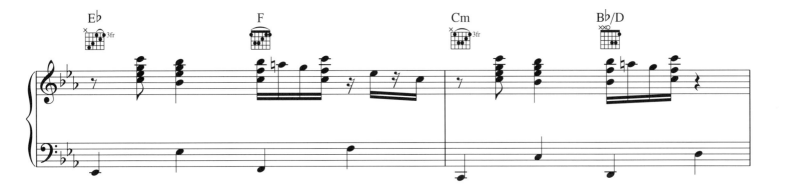

Yeah, yeah, yeah. ____ *(Vocal 1st time only)*

Repeat and Fade **Optional Ending**

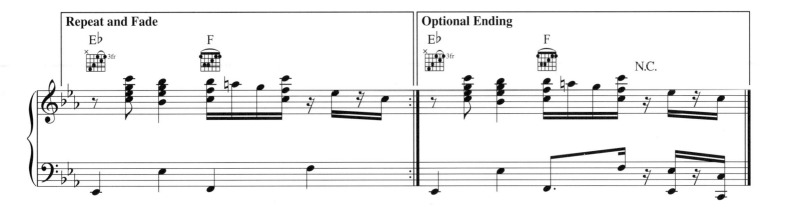

ALL THAT I AM

Words and Music by
ROB THOMAS

I give you all _____ that I am.
I give you all _____ that I am.

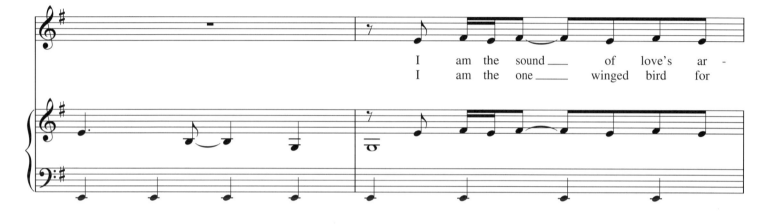

I am the sound _____ of love's ar -
I am the one _____ winged bird for

riv - ing ech-oed soft - ly on the sand. Lay your _ head up-on my
fly - ing, sink-ing quick - ly to the ground. I'm a _____ blind man for a

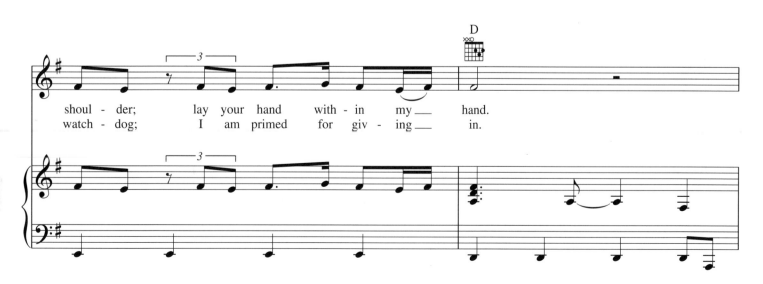

shoul - der; lay your hand with - in my _____ hand.
watch - dog; I am primed for giv - ing _____ in.

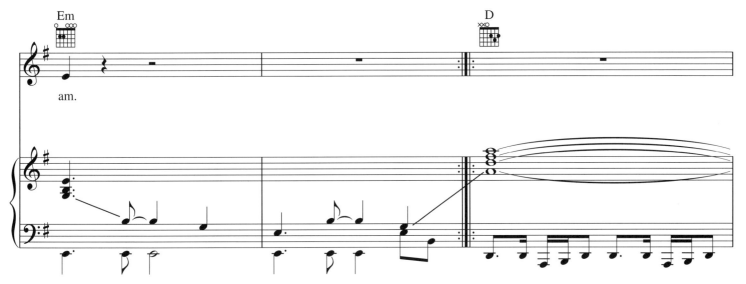

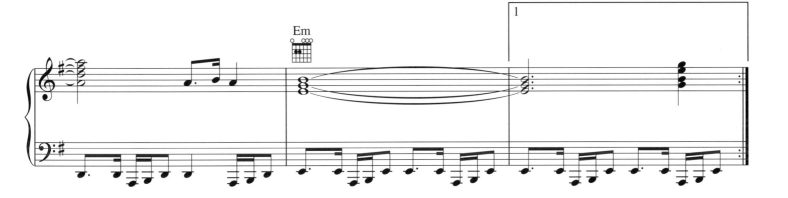

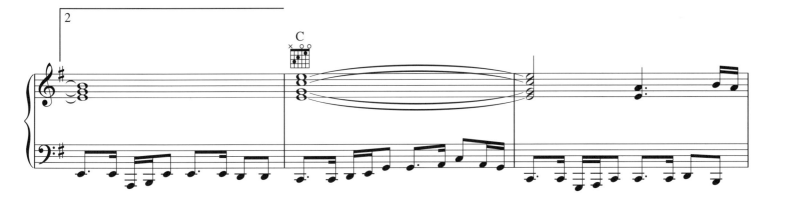

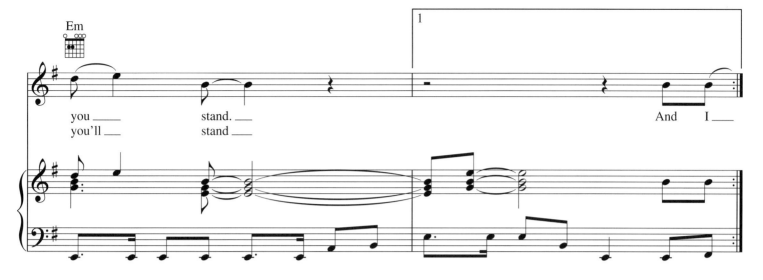

you _____ stand. _____
you'll _____ stand _____
And I _____

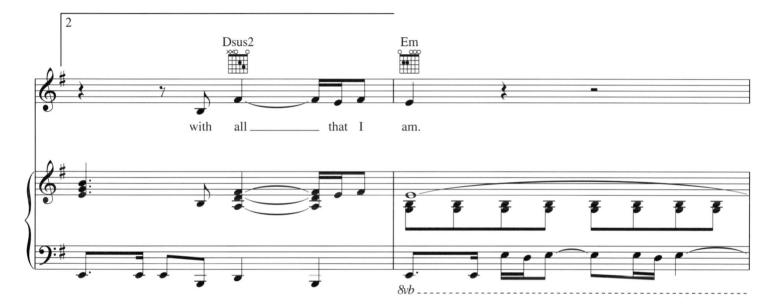

with all _____ that I am.

Play 3 times

PROBLEM GIRL

Words and Music by
ROB THOMAS

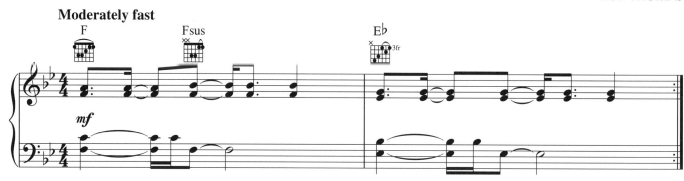

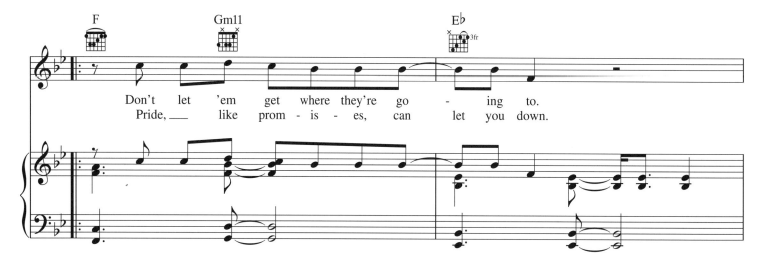

Don't let 'em get where they're go - ing to.
Pride, ___ like prom - is - es, can let you down.

You know they're on - ly what they think of you.
You thought that you'd be feel - ing bet - ter by now, ___

re - mem - ber, you're no prob - lem at all,

you're no prob - lem at all.

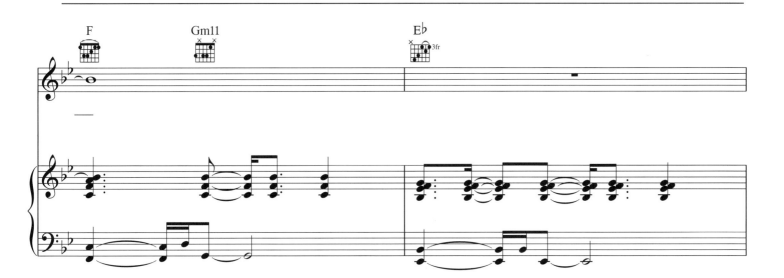

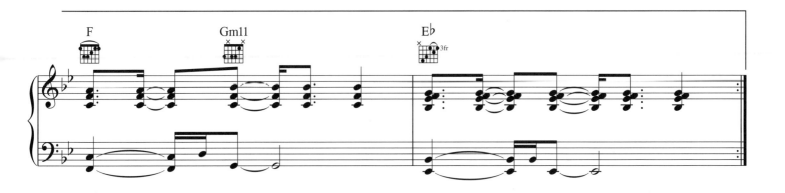

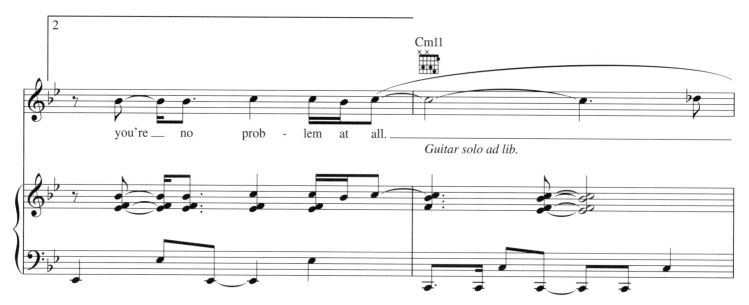

you're __ no prob - lem at all. ___

Guitar solo ad lib.

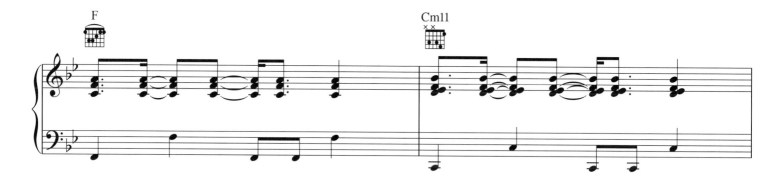

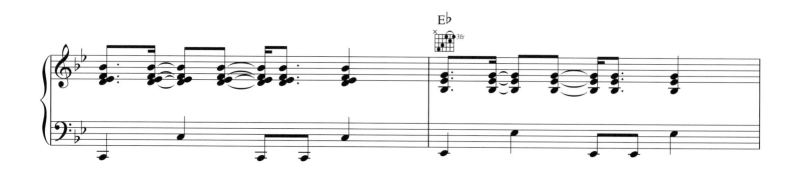

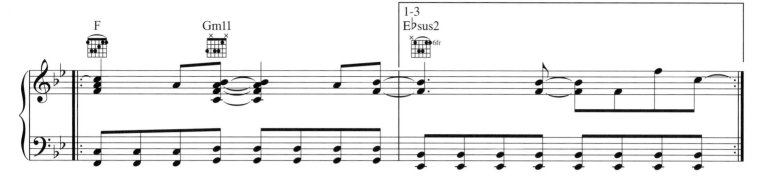

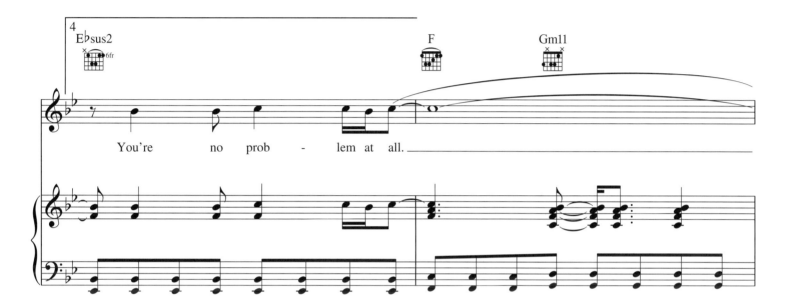

You're no prob - lem at all. ___

FALLIN' TO PIECES

Words and Music by ROB THOMAS
and MATT SERLETIC

un - der way.

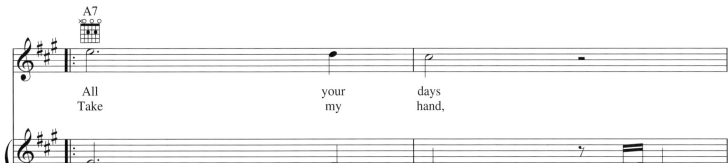

All
Take
your
my
days
hand,

pass
fall
you
in
by.
place.
Sun
Soul
will
in -

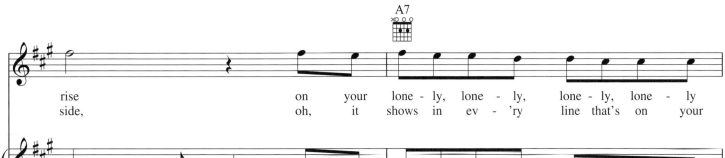

rise
side,
on
oh,
your
it
lone - ly, lone - ly,
shows in ev - 'ry
lone - ly, lone - ly
line that's on your

been a-round town, take it down now, turn a-round. Why is it the ones you love _ that make it all so

hard _ on _ you? Oh, and

then you let it fall be - hind _ and in the back of your mind _ you feel my lov-ing shine; _ you think you might be

saved.

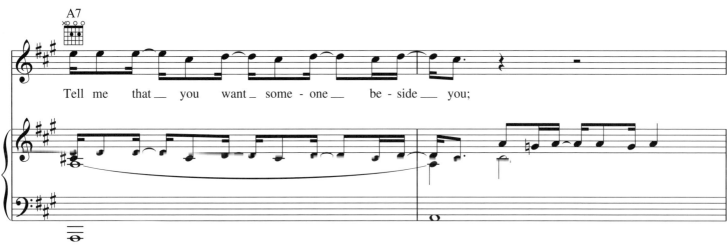

Tell me that __ you want __ some - one __ be - side __ you;

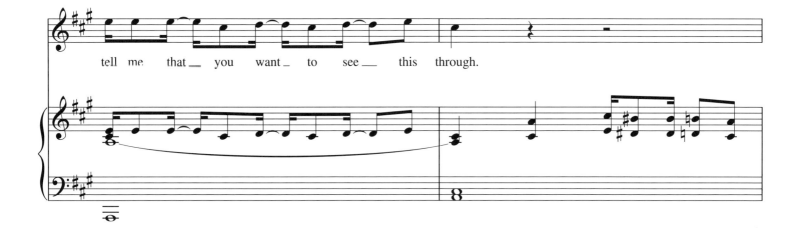

tell me that __ you want __ to see __ this through.

Tell me all the times __ that I've __ been lov - ing you, __ oh, __ you

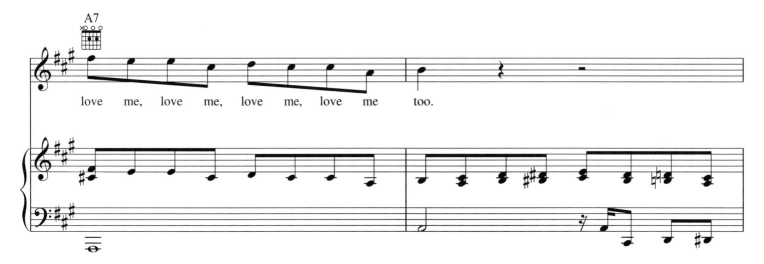

love me, love me, love me, love me too.

Pray _____ just a lit - tle when ev -'ry lit - tle thing starts fall - in' to piec - es. _____

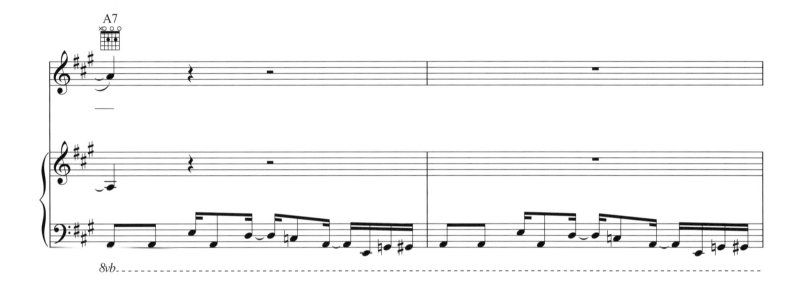

8vb -

(8vb) -

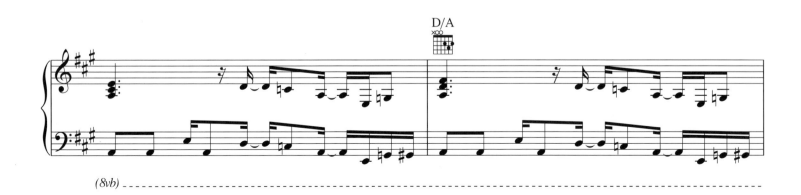

(8vb) -

MY MY MY

Words and Music by
ROB THOMAS

The light from the win - dow is fad - ing; you
Hold on to an - y - thing. Ev - 'ry - thing's

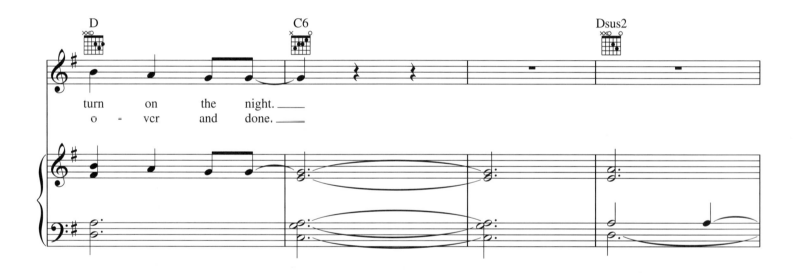

turn on the night. _____
o - ver and done. _____

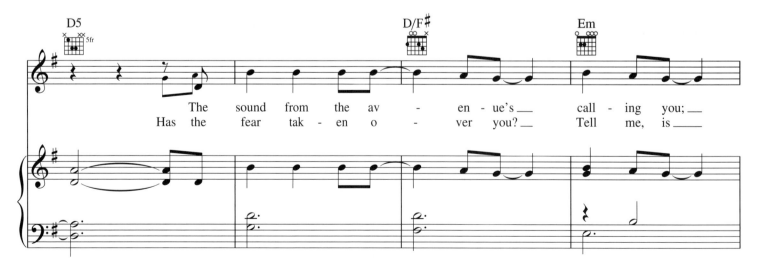

The sound from the av - en - ue's _____ call - ing you; _____
Has the fear tak - en o - ver you? _____ Tell me, is _____

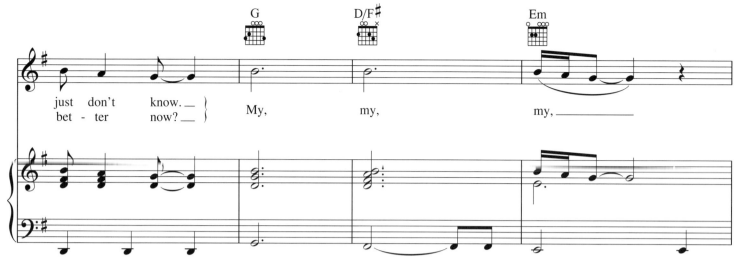

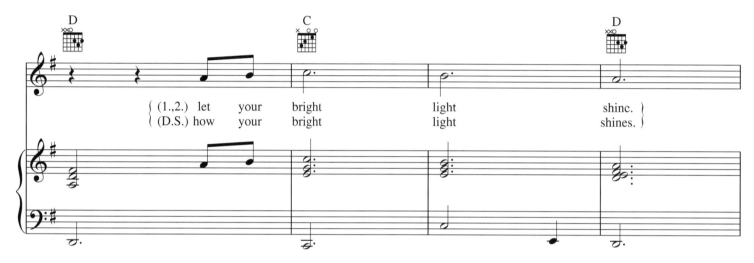

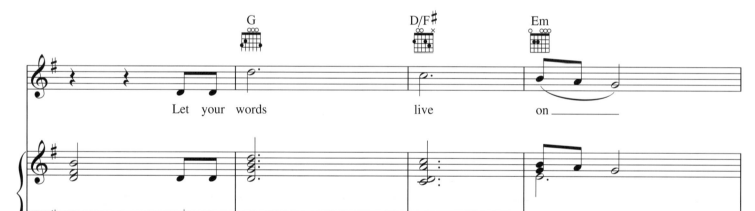

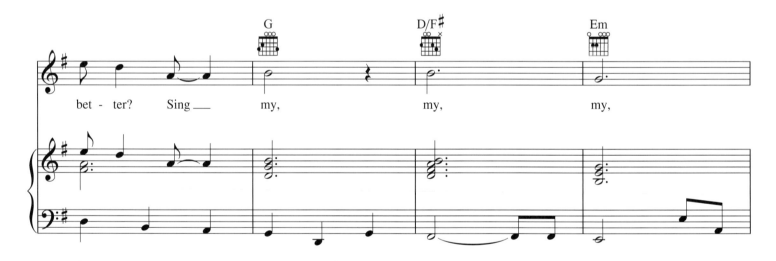

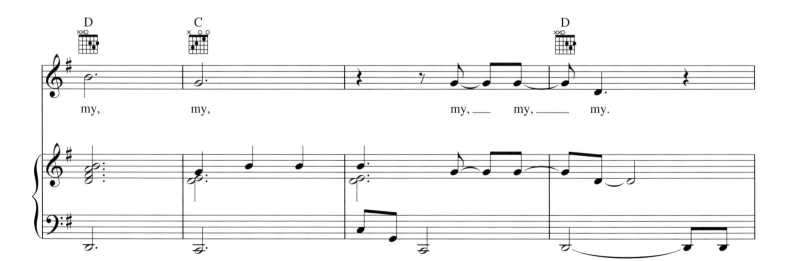

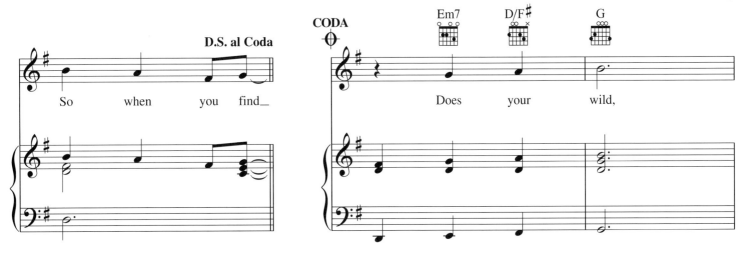

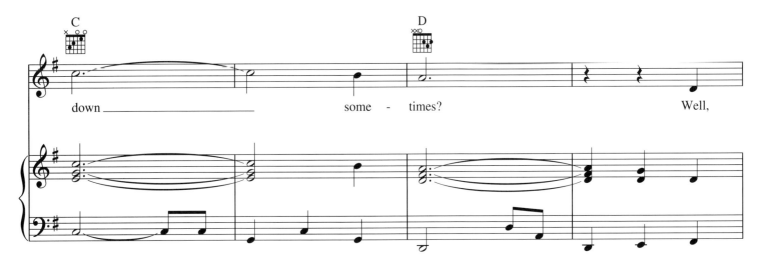

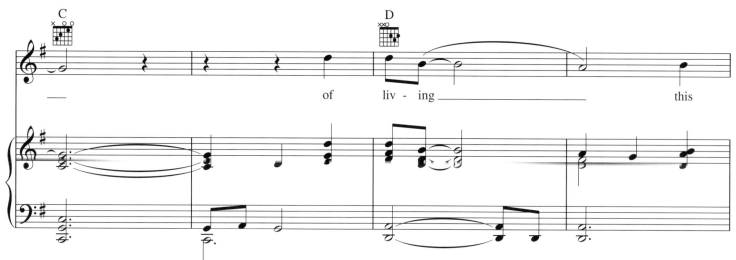

of liv - ing _____ this

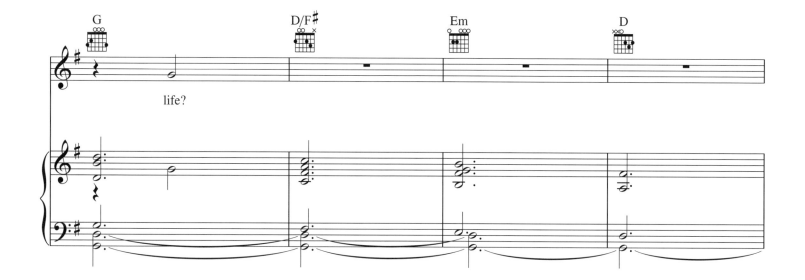

life?

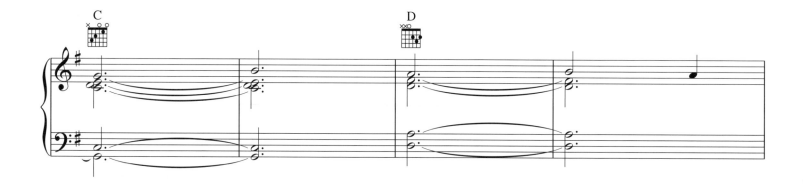

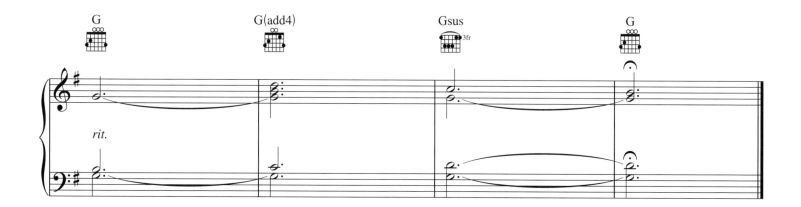

rit.

STREETCORNER SYMPHONY

Words and Music by ROB THOMAS
and MATT SERLETIC

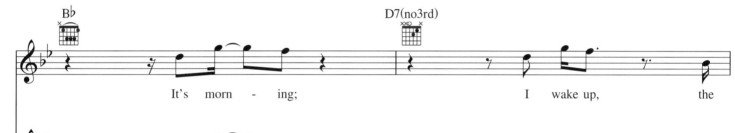

It's morn - ing; I wake up, the

taste of sum - mer sweet - ness on __ my mind.

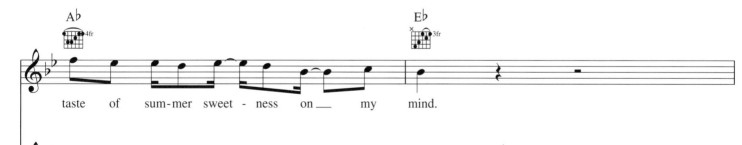

* Recorded one step lower.

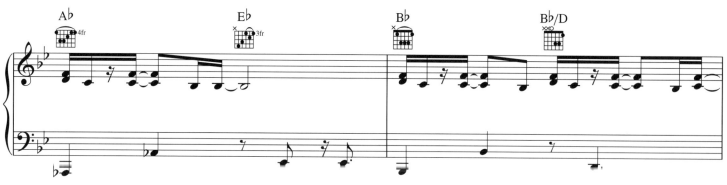

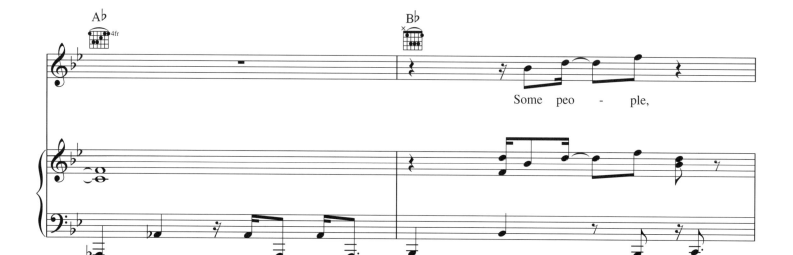

Some peo - ple,

it's __ a pit - y: they go all their lives __ and nev - er know

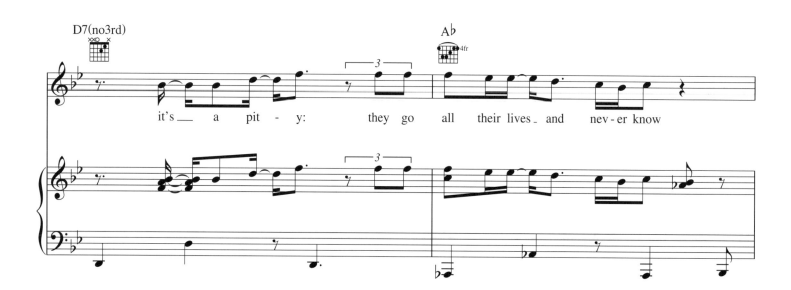

how to love __ or to let __ love go, __ but it's all ____ right now; __ we'll make __

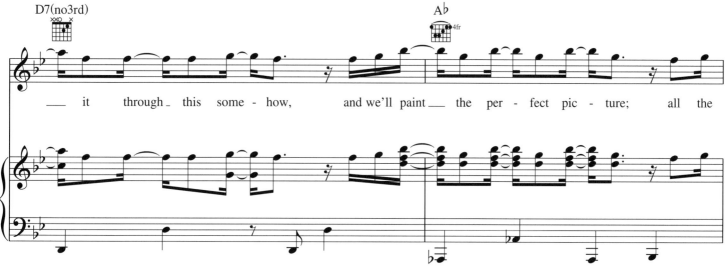

it through this some - how, and we'll paint the per - fect pic - ture; all the

col - ors of this world will run to - geth-

D.S. al Coda

CODA

go, let your - self

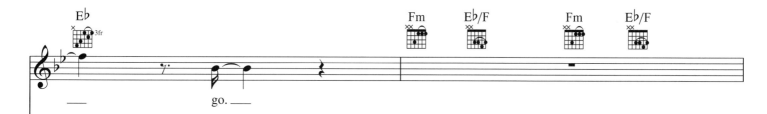

go.

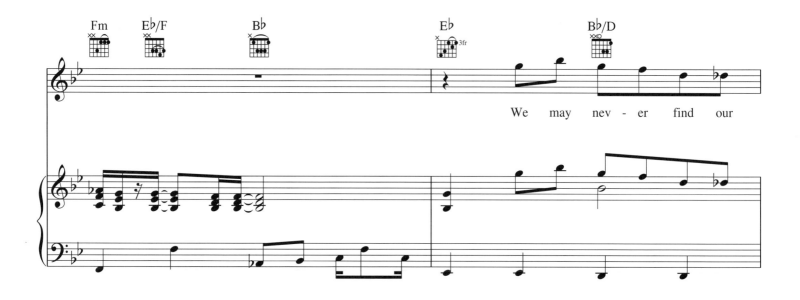

We may nev - er find our

rea - son to shine, ___ but here and now, this is our ___

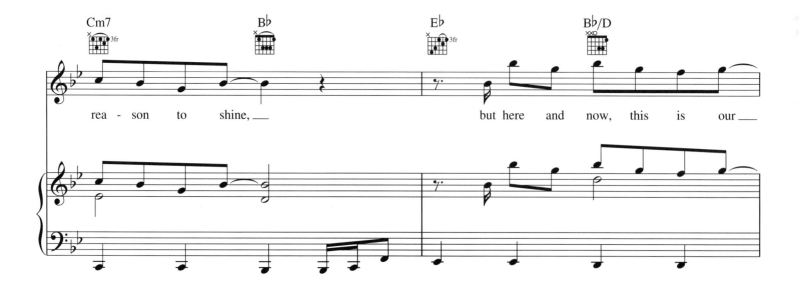

(Yeah, yeah.)
Yeah,__ we go on and on__ and on
On and on__ and on } and on and on and on.__

(Yeah, yeah.)

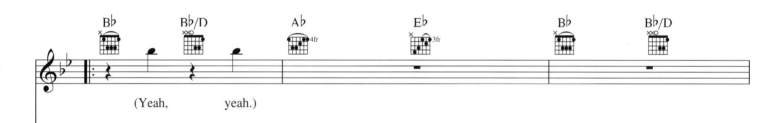

(Yeah, yeah.)

Optional Ending

Repeat and Fade

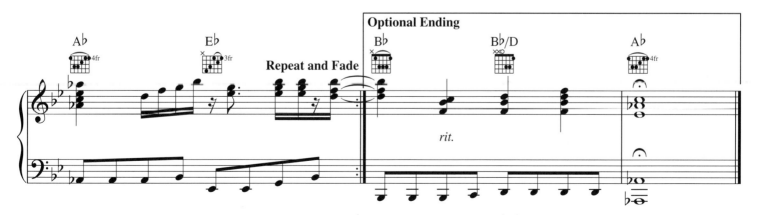

rit.

NOW COMES THE NIGHT

Words and Music by ROB THOMAS
and MATT SERLETIC

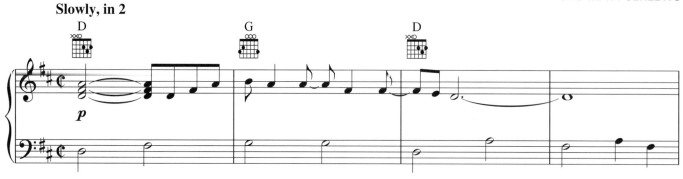

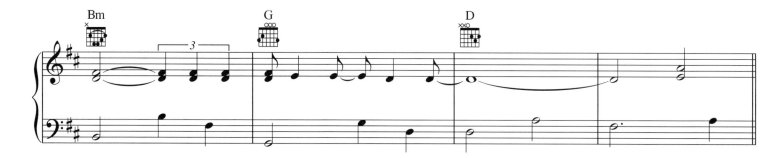

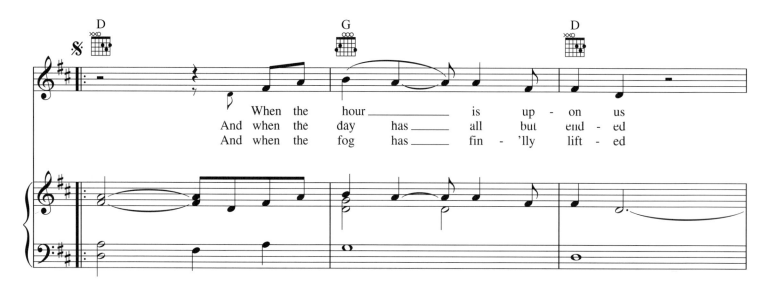

When the hour _____ is up-on us
And when the day has _____ all but end - ed
And when the fog has _____ fin - 'lly lift - ed

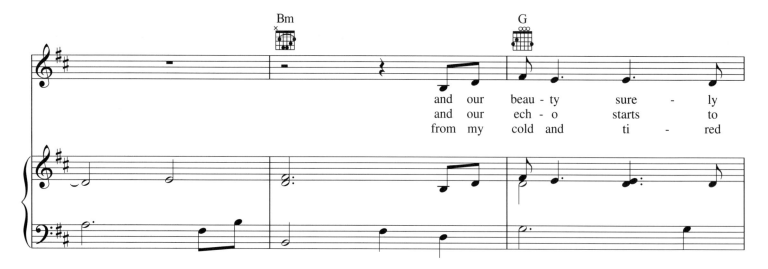

and our beau - ty sure - ly
and our ech - o starts to
from my cold and ti - red

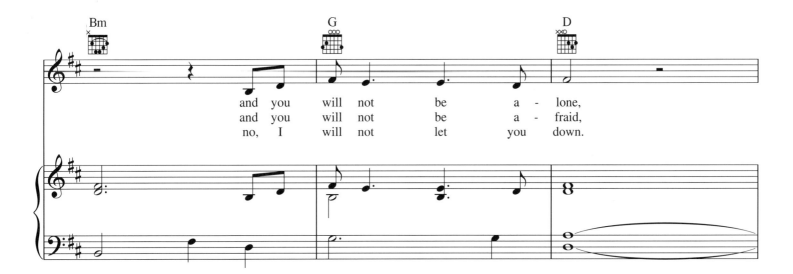

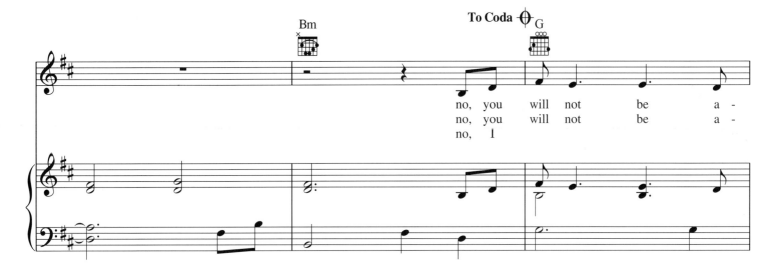

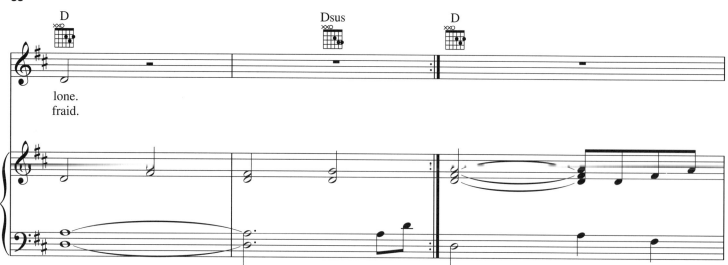

lone.
fraid.

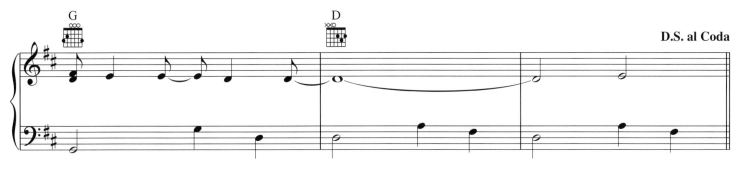

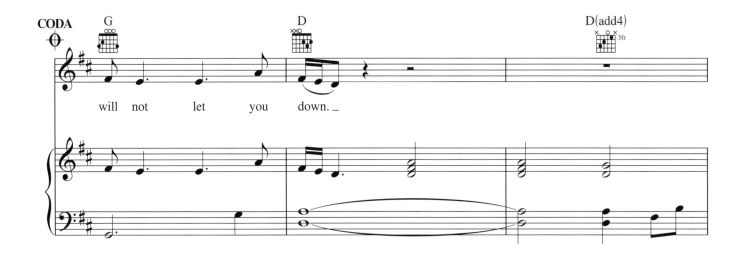

will not let you down. _

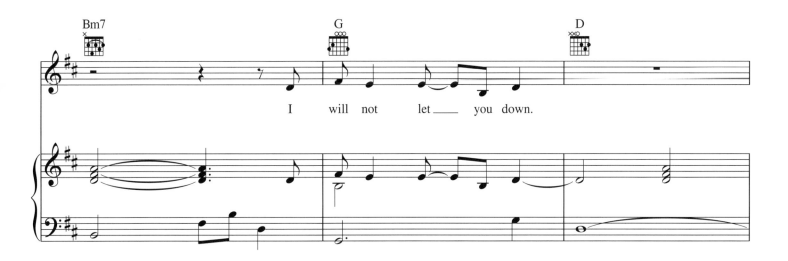

I will not let ____ you down.

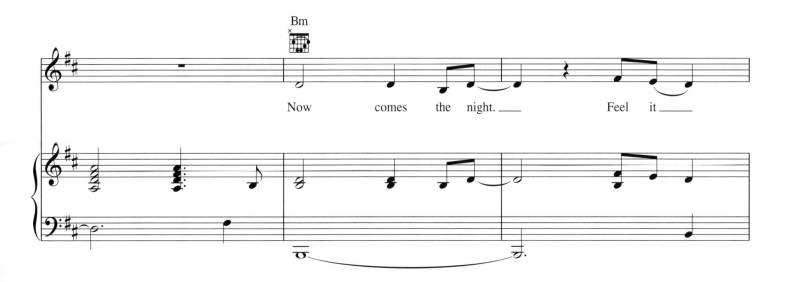

Now comes the night. ____ Feel it ____

end ____ of our days. ____ And when the

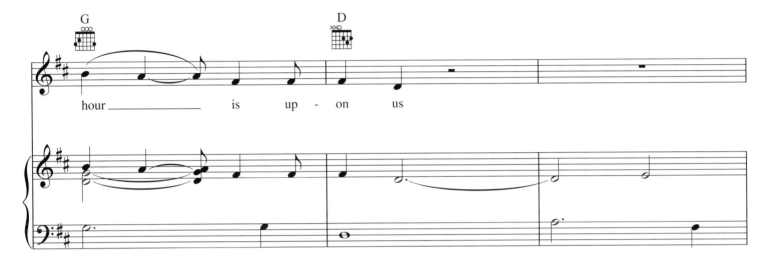

hour _____ is up - on us

and our beau - ty sure - ly gone,

no, you will not be ____ for - got -

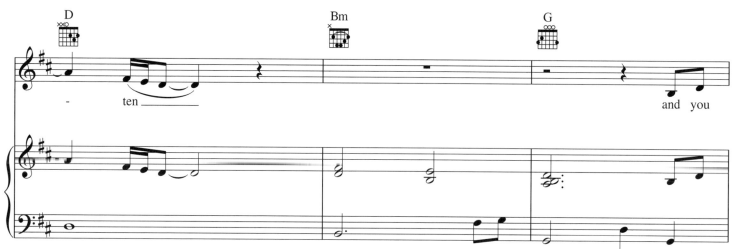

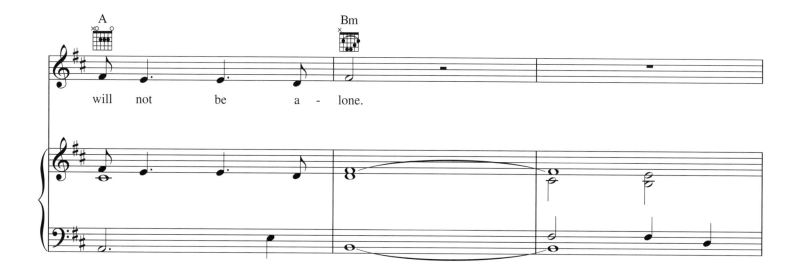

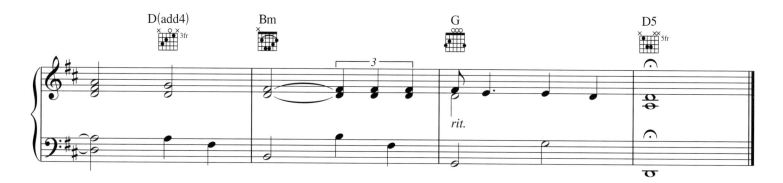